Please visit our web site at: **www.garethstevens.com**
For a free color catalog describing Gareth Stevens Publishing's
list of high-quality books and multimedia programs, call
1-800-542-2595 (USA) or 1-800-387-3178 (Canada).
Gareth Stevens Publishing's fax: (414) 332-3567.

Library of Congress Cataloging-in-Publication Data

Bontinck, Helga.
      At the seashore / Helga Bontinck.—North American ed.
         p. cm. — (Simple steps to drawing)
      Includes bibliographical references.
      ISBN 0-8368-6313-5 (lib. bdg.)
         1. Marine animals in art—Juvenile literature.   2. Seashore in art—Juvenile literature.
      3. Drawing—Technique—Juvenile literature.   I. Title.   II. Series.
      NC781.B66   2006
      743.6—dc22
                                                                              2005040173

This edition first published in 2006 by
Gareth Stevens Publishing
A Member of the WRC Media Family of Companies
330 West Olive Street, Suite 100
Milwaukee, Wisconsin 53212 USA

This U.S. edition copyright © 2006 by Gareth Stevens, Inc. Original edition
copyright © 2005 by Creations for Children International. First published in 2005
by Creations for Children International, Belgium.

All illustrations by Helga Bontinck

Gareth Stevens editor: Dorothy L. Gibbs
Gareth Stevens designer: Scott M. Krall

Printed in the United States of America

1 2 3 4 5 6 7 8 9 10 09 08 07 06

AT THE

Seashore

GARETH**STEVENS**

PUBLISHING

A Member of the WRC Media Family of Companies

EASY DRAWING FUN

This book makes drawing easy, even for little hands. Each left-hand page shows you the shapes, lines, and figures you need to make the colorful drawing you see on the right-hand page. Three easy steps show you how to put the shapes together to make a drawing of a sandcastle, a sailboat, a seagull, or any of six other objects and animals you can find at the seashore.

All you have to do is copy the shapes you see in the first box in the order you see them in the boxes labeled 1, 2, 3. After you finish copying the shapes, you will have a simple drawing that you can color or paint to match the picture in the book — or any other way you like.

Get ready. Get set. **DRAW!**

1 **2** **3**

WHAT YOU WILL NEED

**For drawing, you will need a pencil
and some sheets of plain paper.**

A pencil with soft lead is the best kind for drawing. An ordinary
No. 2 pencil will work well. If you use a pencil that is made
specially for drawing, look for one marked HB. (H means hard lead.
B means soft lead.) A pencil marked HB is not too hard and not too soft.
Use plain white paper for your drawings. The colors and paints
you will use to finish your pictures will show up best on white paper.

**For coloring, you will need crayons,
colored pencils, or markers.
For painting, you will need watercolors
or acrylic or poster paints.**

Crayons and colored pencils are easy to use and come in a wide range of
colors. Markers and paints can be messy so you need to protect your clothing
and your work area. If you want to paint your drawings,
acrylic and poster paints work best because they dry
quickly. You can have a lot of fun mixing paint colors.
Even if you start with only red, blue, yellow, and black
paints, you can mix them to make many other colors.
Paintbrushes come in different thicknesses. You
might want to have two brushes — a thin one and
a thick one. Be sure to wash your brushes in water
when you are finished painting.

Sand Castle

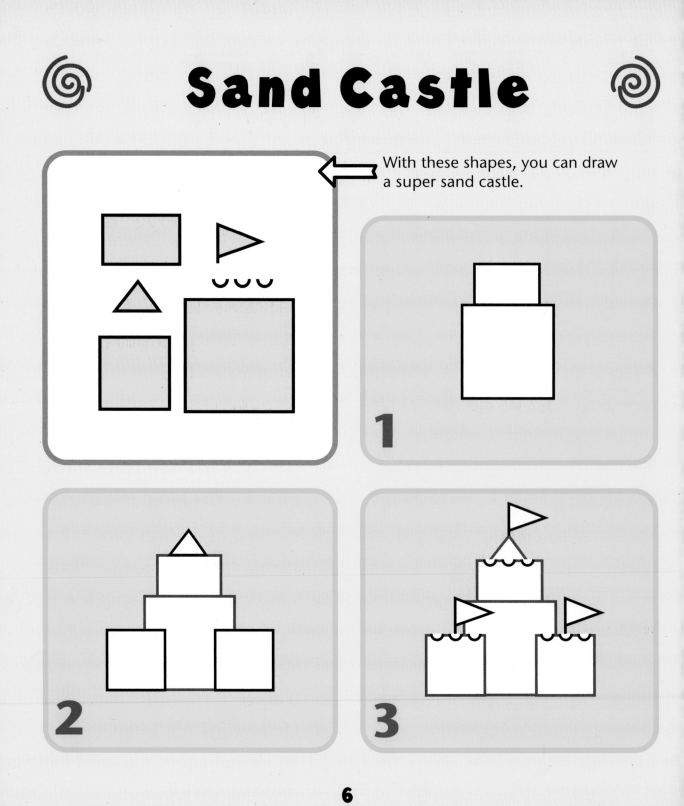

With these shapes, you can draw a super sand castle.

1

2

3

Crab

Use these easy-to-draw figures to make a crab with six legs and two front claws.

1

2

3

Desert Island

A semicircle and three other basic figures are all you need to draw a palm tree on a desert island.

1

2

3

Sailboat

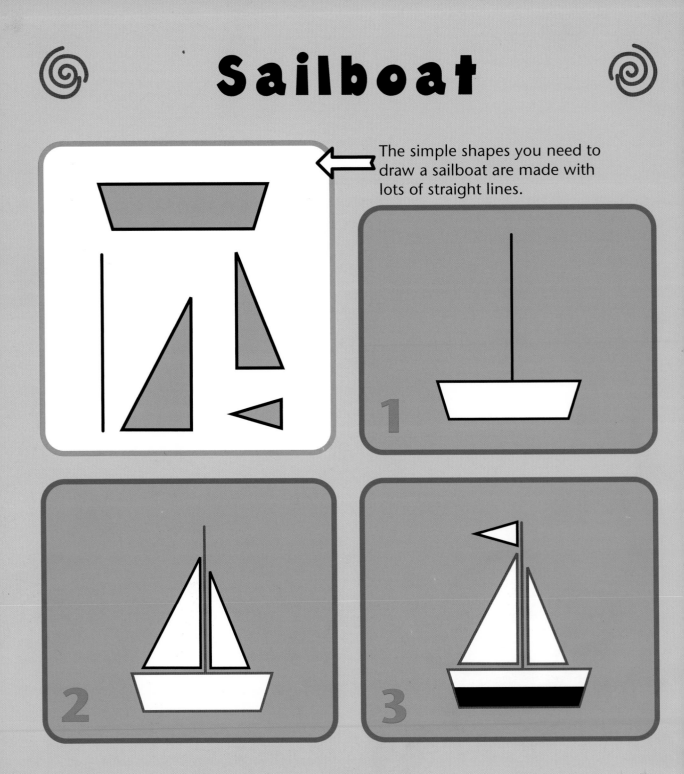

The simple shapes you need to draw a sailboat are made with lots of straight lines.

1

2

3

13

Sea Horse

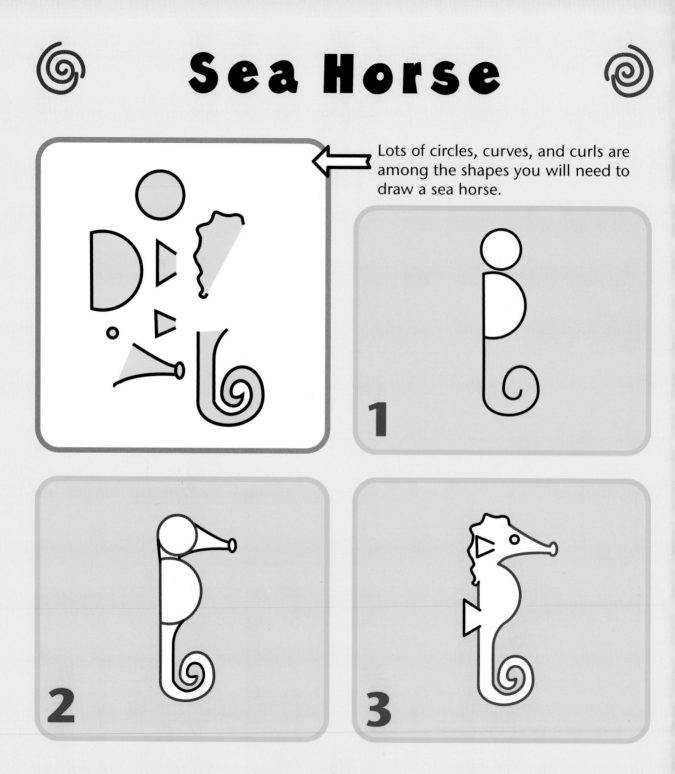

Lots of circles, curves, and curls are among the shapes you will need to draw a sea horse.

1

2

3

Dolphin

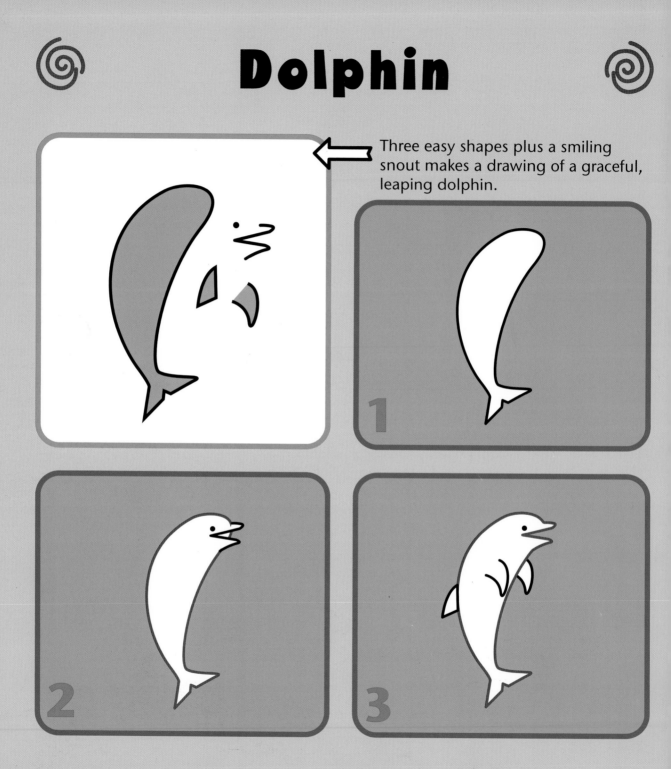

Three easy shapes plus a smiling snout makes a drawing of a graceful, leaping dolphin.

1

2

3

17

Octopus

These circles and squiggles are the main figures you will need to draw an octopus.

1

2

3

19

Seagull

Use this assortment of shapes and figures to draw a standing seagull.

21

Lobster

To draw a lobster, you need circles, ovals, triangles, crescents, spots, and bent lines — like these!

1

2

3

23

MORE EASY DRAWING FUN

Books

Dinosaurs. Easy to Read! Easy to Draw! (series).
   Joan Holub (Price Stern Sloan)

Drawing with Your Hands. Drawing Is Easy (series).
   Godeleine De Rosamel (Gareth Stevens)

I Can Draw Country Animals. I Can Draw Animals! (series).
   Hélène Leroux-Hugon (Gareth Stevens)

Let's Draw a House with Shapes. Let's Draw with Shapes (series).
   Jannel Khu (Rosen's PowerStart Press)

Web Sites

Draw and Color with Uncle Fred
www.unclefred.com

Learn to Draw: A Project 4 Kids
BillyBear4kids.com/Learn2Draw/Learn2Draw.html